Contents

1840

The Light of the Home

PRICE'S CANDLES

93 Honours and Awards

The power cut

The lights went out in the house.

'Power cut,'' shouted Dad.
'Find your torch, Charlie!''

Charlie felt in the cupboard
for his torch.
He switched it on.

'The batteries won't last long,''
he said.

'No,'' said Dad, ''but we can use
the torch to find the candles in
the shed.''

When Dad lit the candles the room looked different, full of shadows.

"This is nice," said Charlie. "Is this how rooms were lit when you and Mum were little?"

Mum laughed. "We're not that old," she said. "We had electric lights. But when Granny was a girl she had gas lights in her house.

She's coming to visit tomorrow, so you must ask her about it."

That night Charlie used a candle to see his way to bed.

"What are candles made of?" he asked.

"Paraffin wax," said Mum. "It's made from oil—the kind you get from oil wells under the ground or under the sea.

Candles are made in a candle factory.

A hundred years ago there were lots of candle factories.

Now there's only one in Britain because nearly everyone has electric light."

The Light of the Home

PRICE'S CANDLES

93 Honours and Awards

Price's Candles advertisement, 1840

"A long time ago, people quite often made candles at home," said Mum.

"Some were made of meat fat. They were called tallow candles.

Fat was saved from the cooking. It was melted and poured into a candle mould. A wick was put in the mould too. When the fat got cold it went hard and made a candle.

The new candles were kept in a box on the wall so they didn't catch fire by mistake.

Some candles were made of beeswax—that's what bees make their honeycombs from.

They were the most expensive kind. When they burned they smelt like honey.

Tallow candles were cheaper but they were smoky and didn't smell so nice."

Welsh women making tallow candles, c. 190C

"Another way to make candles is to dip them," said Mum.

"The wick is just a piece of twisted cotton. If you keep dipping it into melted wax you can build up the candle in layers.

Blists Hill Museum Candle Factory

Some candle factories had special machines called 'nodding donkeys' that dipped the candles in and out of the wax.''

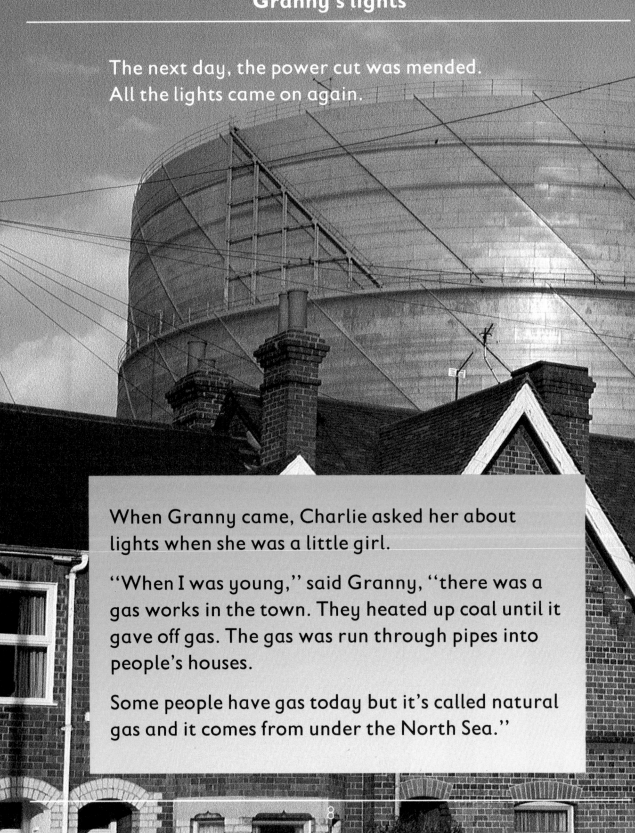

The next day, the power cut was mended.
All the lights came on again.

When Granny came, Charlie asked her about lights when she was a little girl.

"When I was young," said Granny, "there was a gas works in the town. They heated up coal until it gave off gas. The gas was run through pipes into people's houses.

Some people have gas today but it's called natural gas and it comes from under the North Sea."

"In my home we didn't have any electric lights," said Granny.

"The gas pipes went up the wall and at the end of them was a switch and a burner called a mantle. You switched on the gas and lit the mantle with a match."

"Was it dangerous?" asked Charlie.

"A bit," said Granny. "The gas was poisonous so if there was a leak, it made people ill. Sometimes it exploded too. We had a gas meter in the front room to pay for the gas."

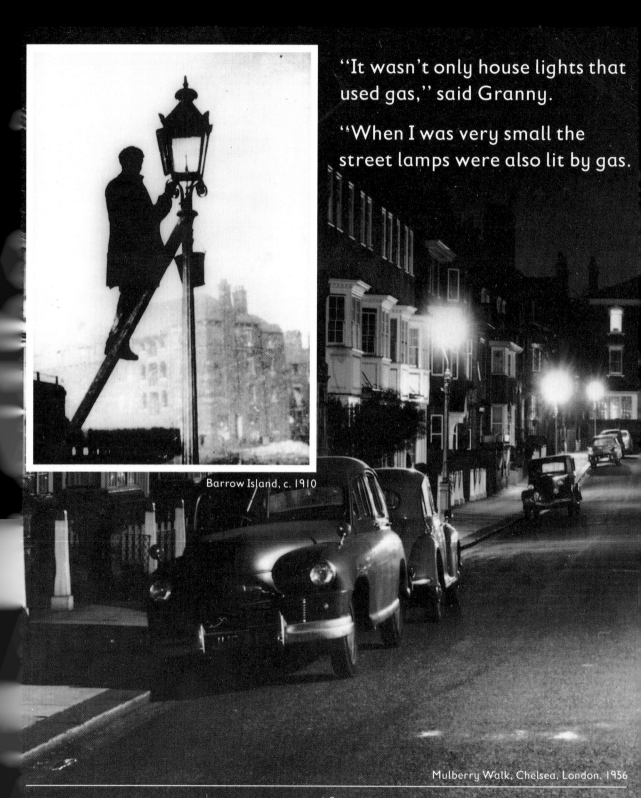

"It wasn't only house lights that used gas," said Granny.

"When I was very small the street lamps were also lit by gas.

Barrow Island, c. 1910

When it got dark a lamplighter would come round with an oil lamp on the end of a long pole.

He turned on the gas at each street lamp and then lit it.

I loved to watch the lamplighter."

Oil lamps

"Lots of people didn't have gas or electricity at home," said Granny.

"How did they see in the dark?" asked Charlie.

"They used oil lamps.

Lightmoor, near Ironbridge, Shropshire, 1953

My Uncle Fred lived in the country. It was too far from the gas works to have gas lights. He used lamps that were filled with paraffin oil.

It wasn't a very bright light. If you wanted to read in the evening you had to move close to the lamp."

Then Charlie's Dad found a picture of a room nearly two hundred years ago.

"Look at this, Charlie," he said. "Do you think this lady had electricity in her home—or gas or oil?"

"She had candles," said Charlie. "I can see the candlesticks."

Cottage interior, Compton Basset, by Elizabeth Pearson Dalby, 1849

"What are those things that look like scissors?" asked Mum.

"They're snuffers," said Dad. "Sometimes the candle wick got too long and started to smoke so they used the snuffers to trim the wick."

The tinder box

Next day they went to the museum.
Charlie saw lots of things to do with lights.

The first thing was a little round metal box in one
of the cases. Inside it was a piece of flint and
a piece of steel. In the bottom of the box were
some tiny bits of cloth.

"It's a tinder box," said Dad. "This is how people
lit their candles before matches were invented.
They hit the steel against the flint till it made a
spark which fell on the cloth in the box and set
it alight".

"That sounds like fun," said Charlie.

"Not if you were in a hurry!" said Dad.

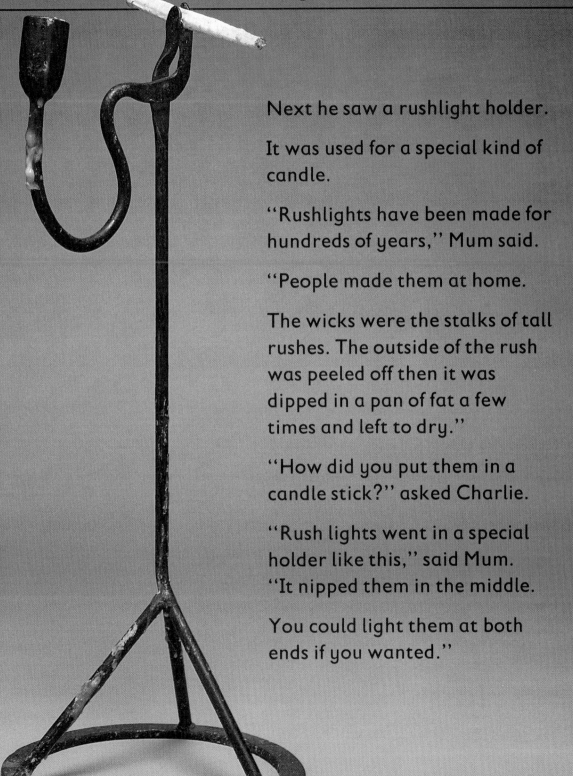

Next he saw a rushlight holder.

It was used for a special kind of candle.

"Rushlights have been made for hundreds of years," Mum said.

"People made them at home.

The wicks were the stalks of tall rushes. The outside of the rush was peeled off then it was dipped in a pan of fat a few times and left to dry."

"How did you put them in a candle stick?" asked Charlie.

"Rush lights went in a special holder like this," said Mum. "It nipped them in the middle.

You could light them at both ends if you wanted."

Miners' lamps

Davy Lamp,
Ashington Colliery,
Northumberland, 191

Charlie also saw some miners' lamps.

Mum said, "Miners who work underground need lamps to see by.

Until two hundred years ago they used candles but these sometimes caused explosions because of gas coming from the coal.

A man called Davy invented a special safety lamp. It was an oil lamp which had wire gauze around the flame. It only gave a dim light but it stopped explosions in the mines. It saved a lot of lives and was sometimes called the 'miner's friend'.

Today, miners have a torch with batteries fitted into their helmets."

Houghton Main Colliery, Yorkshire

In one of the cases Charlie saw a lantern with a thick round piece of glass at the front.

"It's a bull's eye lantern," said Dad. "Policemen used to carry them at night.

The thick piece of glass is called a lens. It magnified the candle flame inside and directed it into a strong beam."

"It's like the torches we use today," said Charlie. "Only it has a candle inside, not a battery."

London, Gustav Doré, 1872

At school on Monday, everybody talked about the storm and the power cut.

Miss Tomlinson, the teacher, said that she didn't have any candles at home so she used a hurricane lamp.

"What's a hurricane lamp?" shouted everybody.

"It's sometimes called a storm lamp," she said, "You fill it with paraffin oil and light the wick. It has glass around it so it won't blow out. You can take it outside even in a strong wind and it will stay alight.

You used to be able to buy them in hardware shops just like you buy torches today."

Yoxall Village stores. Reconstruction in the Staffordshire County Museum

"There are lots of different kinds of lamps and lanterns," said Miss Tomlinson.

She showed the class a picture of old candle lanterns. They were made so that the candle would not blow out.

"Let's make a collection," she said.
"Bring in as many lights as you can from home.
"I'll bring in my hurricane lamp tomorrow."

The collection

The next day the classroom looked like a museum.

There were lots of different candlesticks.
Some were metal, some were wood and
some were china.

Bertie brought in an old bicycle lamp
called a carbide lamp.
He found it in his Grandad's shed.

Charlie took in his torch.

Brian had some old fairy lights.

The Roman lamp

Miss Tomlinson held up the Roman lamp.

"This is what the Romans used about two thousand years ago.

This one is a copy but it looks just like the lamps that have been dug up on the site of Roman houses.

It was filled with olive oil. A wick was put down the spout and lit."

Emily had a carriage lantern that was used on a pony cart.

Luke showed them a copy of a Roman lamp that he had bought on holiday.

The carbide lamp

Mr Warren, the school caretaker, came in to tell the children about Bertie's carbide lamp.
He could remember people using them when he was young.

The children looked inside.

"This is a gas lamp, really," Mr Warren said. "You put some powder called calcium carbide inside. Then you filled the top with water.

c. 1920

When the water dripped on the carbide it gave off a gas.

The gas came through a little burner and you lit i with a match.

It gave out a good light until the carbide powder was all used up."

World War II poster

Mr Warren said, "When I was a boy it was wartime.

All the street lights were turned off so enemy planes couldn't see the towns.

At night time we covered our windows with wooden frames filled with brown paper so that no light could be seen outside.

All our curtains were lined with black material.

It was called 'the blackout'.

You couldn't even strike a match outdoors.

We carried white handkerchieves when we went out so people could see us."

The children made drawings of all the lights in the collection. Next they sorted out the pictures.

Then Miss Tomlinson made a timeline to peg up the pictures in order.

At one end she pegged up the picture of the Roman lamp because it was two thousand years old. At the other end she pegged up a picture of an electric light bulb.

In between, the children pegged up all their other pictures of candles, gas lights and tinderboxes.